The Alchemist's Daughter

Dylan Catherine

Presentation by *BookLeaf Publishing*

Web: www.bookleafpub.com

E-mail: info@bookleafpub.com

ISBN: 9789363307674

First edition 2024

*I dedicate this to every version of me: past,
present, future.*

no cup is big enough for my sadness...

though formless her body rests
heavy in my chest while I ache and
through my veins she colors my skin and
she seeps through my pores while I cry out
"I can't see you when my vision is blurry!"

I hope to pour her into something so that
she may become more tangible and
maybe then I'd understand her better
but for now I will carry her within me

quietly and carefully

The Alchemist's Daughter

My daddy thinks he has the Midas touch;
That, to strike gold, willpower is enough.

He hurt me to make me better, he said;
Where I should have been held, he bruised
instead.

Diminish my sense of self, that was key;
Subject to a cruel kind of alchemy.

My body, now covered in gilded scars,
He thought what was mine would always be
ours.

Molded by a love that was counterfeit,
I'm not his precious metal to covet.

Inner Child

My grief is a garden, untended.
Long overgrown and invading
Where I once buried a body.

I visit often, but never at night.
I am no bone collector, but
I brought a shovel with me this time.

The center of the earth has a heartbeat.
And it's been calling out to me, so
I resolve to dig deeper until...

The girl I used to be, now disinterred,
Sobs as I brush the dirt off her face.
"You never stop crying." I say.

"I only ever wanted someone to hear me."

"I'm so sorry I stopped listening."

"That's okay, I knew you'd come back
someday."

I ache to bring her home again, but
We both know this is her final resting place.

I'm grown now and I need to let this be.

I tuck her back into the ground, and
Wrapped up in my goodbye kiss is
A promise to tend to the garden again.

Because of the tears we have collected,
Soon, flowers will bloom where she lays.
That's when I know we'll both be forgiven.

The Alchemist's Father

In poetry I can make believe
My daddy is an alchemist.
Instead, the truth is this:
My daddy is a narcissist.

I'd much rather play pretend
I was the sorcerer's apprentice,
But my daddy was no teacher,
He was just a cruel life lesson.

But, I sometimes like to think that,
If my daddy taught me anything,
It was how to take all of my pain
And turn it into poetry like magic.

I guess that makes alchemy my birthright.

A Life Spent Evaporating
(Candle Magic)

My heart only knows envy
'Cause the best is the only
Acceptable way to be

And now I can only burn
My body from both ends to
Be seen as exceptional

The wax melts green…

Law of Attraction

Most of the time I blame myself for the tension.
Wondering still, do you ever feel it?
The truth is that I wished for this.
Crossing my fingers every time
I said I loved him.

Big Bang Theory

"Your eyes are alight like fireworks," she said.
Hot flashes in the colorburst, burning.
She sees a universe inside my head;
The product of a feverish yearning.
My gaze turns over. I am red like Mars.
In my dreams I can touch her without fear.
Her silhouette, a collection of stars.
Constellations of memories held dear.
And yet, my heart burns brighter out of spite.
In the heat of collapse, I feel the rift.
This isn't love, it's a nuclear light
To be seen years from now; a Doppler shift.
Black hole imagination, from the void
I created something to be destroyed.

Orange Crush

I fell for a boy when I was fourteen
He always shared his lunch with me
But it only made me more hungry

I imagined that he would taste sweet
Like orange crush and vanilla ice cream
The sugar cravings always made me dizzy

I was greedy then, I didn't want to share
I made a mess of things and I didn't care
In the end, I took my sticky hands elsewhere

Sirena

My disco-dyed fantasy
Colored seafoam green

She speaks to me in cursive
With a crooked tongue

Laying bare in the wet grass
Like blades in our backs

I read in between the lines
Through moonlit kisses

The taste of her still lingers
On each bitter breath

A love that feels like drowning
That is what we have

Red Thumb

With ruddy hands I lay to rest the kisses that you
stole
Each one buried deep in the earth of my breast

And after the storm, my flesh is tender topsoil
Bloodrich and yielding an ironic bloom
For future lovers to prune, pick, and pull at
My once reclaimed network of arteries

But I know that the bruises are proof
That my heart has not hardened

Sad Dream

Baby bunny burrows in my belly
Seeking a short-term refuge
I pray my body is a sanctuary
I would be grateful to hold
Something warm for once

Yellow (Waking Up)

Rancid, choleric
The color, I can smell it
My skin when I'm sick

Grief is a Secret that I Keep

It's skipping a meal
Before I let myself eat

(later)

It's turning the music up
Before I let myself cry

(finally)

It's watching the sunrise
Before I let myself rest

Resentment

It's easier to confess my love
Than it is my disappointment.

What comes first?
The sadness or anger?
Whichever it is, it sticks
To the back of my throat;
A painful infection that
Is treatment resistant.

Yellow (Throwing Up)

Mouth tastes like poison
Bilirubin in my blood
I need to vomit

Tonsillectomy

The carpet ripples in the room my daddy used to
play video games in.
Heavier remembering the summer after first
grade, when
The doctors told me not to speak, so we laughed
instead.

Standing in the same spot I used to watch over
his left shoulder,
Where the floor bubbles under the weight of me
now, I wonder…

Did he mistake my rasping then
For his own demons mocking?

Is that why we grew up yelling?
Is that why he never believed a word I said?
Had we not broken the rules in the first place,
Would every "I love you" have sounded so harsh
After nineteen years of shouting?

I stifle my coughs and swallow each question in
the quiet.
Although my throat still itches today, we haven't
spoken in years.

I feel that familiar burn, thinking about how
much it hurts.

I can't wait to rip out the carpet in here.

Metastasis

As my cells divide and multiply
It's no wonder I feel so heavy

Deep in my telomeres
My father's indignation
My mother's isolation

Echoes of a pain that came before me
Send signals to the rest of my body

Not enough
Not enough
Not enough

The messages resonate
My brain, my blood, my bones
All of me must compensate

Yellow (Giving Up)

Emergency room
Crying while I wait my turn
I want this to end

The greatest tragedy is that…

I'll always love you to capacity.
I begged for your intimacy, yet you
misunderstood.
Now, the physical distance will make up the
difference.
A legacy of grief, wrapped up in the sound of
each other's name,
Carries on in our shared selfishness because you
will never know my children.

Canonization

I keep every love note like a book of prayers
Paper confessions, twice-torn and taped-over
Sometimes I wish I wasn't so sentimental
Maybe then I wouldn't let myself believe
Everyone I ever loved who also hurt me
Was meant to make me a martyr

Resignation of Self-Love

Fine! If you don't want it then
I will take all of this love that I carry,
Boundless and burdensome yards
Of tender threads, unraveling
And reweave myself into
My cocoon heart

9 789363 307674